EMPOWER

A Book of Life, Peace and Love

Copyright by Luis Stefanell 2017©
All Rights Reserved
Decatur, Georgia

Contact Information
Luis Stefanell
P. O. Box 692
Decatur, Georgia 30031
404-377-3112

stefanellluis@gmail.com
fb.me/empower

This book is dedicated to "Toonces"
The Cat, not only any cat but Christy Emory's cat!
At nineteen we know you had to go away, Christy misses you every day!
Long live the memory of your meows!

This book is dedicated to you the readers and all on life's journey!

My friends that know my spirit know that I at times take full advantage of my voice, it is my birthright to do so. I see it as in part of my years as a musician where I am simply expressive making music for others to enjoy. Writing of my beliefs, my thoughts give me a certain sense of gratification. Mostly knowing others relate and enjoy what I have to share with them. I hope this offering does in fact inspire, move and lift your heart!

Luis Stefanell

Acknowledgement

I would like to thank once again my friends at Decatur Atlanta Printing, Mr. Martin Terry, Mr. Mike Wilson and staff and Ms. Sandy Bishop for your consideration always to serve me well with my projects to get my messages of how wonderful this life in fact is!

Thank you all!

I would like to take this moment to thank you for your interest in having this book. Thank you!

At the completion and release of my second book *The Message 2016 (A Book of Poetry, Spoken Word and Art)* I found myself picking up my pen and doing it all over again . . . "hey" that rhymed!

I thought I would offer myself a break from writing and 'all that goes into' putting what I envision as my work to offer.

But 'creative spirit doesn't rest' this is why it should be guided is what I mentioned in my first book "Love Endlessly" 2014. And as the saying goes 'strike when the iron's hot' so I did and this is the result.

I like to be expressive and what better subject to write about than life itself!

There is so much I want to say and share with others. I enjoy the process of thinking, writing and sculpting thoughts and words to convey what is within me.

I love the Creative Arts!

I am primarily a musician– a percussionist for most of my life but this is becoming a close first!

Yes, I have had others before, I have had wonderful days in the past and that goes without saying but this moment is very special, because I know these works (books) are being appreciated by others.

continued

There is absolutely nothing better I could share with another than to know there is something I've written that is moving in some way.

'Yes' music does carry me away but to know the life of another can be positively affected in some way means much to me.

So again I would like to express my gratitude for your interest in being interested in this book. May it inspire you and lift your heart in some positive way forever in a day!

Thank you!
Luis Stefanell

celebrate

A Child's Eyes

I often wonder how children must see this world, at times it must seem just 'Wild'! With what they see and hear I imagine it to be at times confusing. From fun loving to chaotic to all in between adventures– discoveries– joys– mysteries– sorrows– to even fearful events who knows what's in store for tomorrow.

A calming kind peaceful Love is something they can relate to. It's what makes them feel blessed in this chess– game of life.

I Love life!

And as you might imagine by now, I spend many a moment enjoying working at figure it out and understand situations that occur, I believe we all do, some more than others.

Through the years some of my friends have mentioned to me that I should write a book on my life, and for a moment think to myself 'that would be boring' and part self-serving. And each time I think and reply I would rather write something about all of us (our behavior) for others including myself. I believe that would be more interesting. We all think and feel and have the same emotions– thoughts at different times but perhaps in slightly different ways.

I Love this life on loan granted to me to live out, I see the gift that it is! There are so many things that fascinate me

and have to work to understand other circumstances that arise that challenge me.

continued

If you think about it there are 'three basic things' everyone desires in life. One is to be acknowledged, Two to be accepted as they are, and Three to be loved for who they are. With these basic qualities in our minds we can go far in relationships as simple as they are. Any one of them is important in being effective for all relationships.

Everyone has something to offer others more than one may know, we all are one another's spirit guide– teachers. Making intentional contact with others is important in the area of exchange – sharing, kindness and Love.

Drawing one another in 'is the start of something good' that could occur. We are created to share in all the wonderful things this life has to offer.

So for me these 'basic three thing' are always important to keep in the front of my mind.

Rejection isn't something I have to deal with, or 'concern myself with'. If I offer– give and someone isn't receptive, I just leave it there. I do my best as not to impose of myself to others. My giving is a one way offering. A love energy which is designed to be so. My kindness and Love energy is the most powerful thing– offering I possess to share with all.

Remember, Love's the word!

The Children

A child has a chance given one.

    A child may not know which way to go that's why it looks– it seeks guidance.

But it does know to wait.

    It knows not much but the most important, which is to simply Love.

We are the children looking to restore hope for an even better world.

Under The Sky

If I'm not using my mind I must be wasting time!

You see I believe it all starts there . . .

To where and what I'll do next paint art,

play music write a poem– song

or just sit in reflection or even better no

thought in mind that's also where I find myself in time.

I like it all, I like to dine on all the gifts under the sky!

Given In Peace

Peaceful spirit

Peaceful mind

Peace is given

Peace I find!

Aspire

I aspire to be the best I can be.

I aspire to search and see all of life's beauty.

I aspire to reach higher then higher.

I aspire to give more, then even more as I continue to live!

I aspire to learn that which interest me and to share it as I move along.

Of all that I aspire, I aspire to continue to be peaceful, kind and God Loving to all!

divine

Emotions Motions

Can you put a price on emotions?

Can you put a price on feeling well, feeling good? No I don't think so!

There is no monetary price one could place on this emotion of an up-beat nature. The first thing that comes to mind is that it is earned– achieved by taking care of oneself, taking care of your well being.

Not everyone is always up-beat, we all fluctuate with ups and downs. The thing is to monitor one's demeanor, attitude moment-to-moment and make adjustments. By doing so things tend to flow and move along more naturally. Emotions don't lie!

Things come to you more naturally, people are drawn to you because you help bring out the best in them when in an up beat mode . . . 'Good things happen'! Things get done!

When in a 'down' moment we should examine ourselves to pin point what has placed us there, what reaction did we take to place ourselves feeling like this, after all we are responsible for all of our emotions and not others. It's how I react to things that will determine how things will go.

Personally, I find myself centering myself when I feel the need to do so. This creates a turnaround in the way of 'me' controlling my emotions and acts from my higher thought. Situations, events, people can, at times, throw me off and I

continued

need to stay focused to see things through well, so my emotions can come into play and I guide myself as well as I can. I do this first by observing my thoughts, speak slowly and watch my responding words if and when communicating with others.

It all starts in the mind 'to be mindful'.

We are emotional beings with our minds leading the way, our path. I believe the more one practices guiding thoughts consistently life just seems to flow naturally. The key word for all of this is to be 'positive in mind'. To be sure the outcome will be one of desire. Something I know will manifest to my liking.

We are our best healers, leaders!

No one knows you better than you know yourself! In my book I've mentioned the benefits of meditations, it can't be said enough to center the body and mind this is a wonderful thing to incorporate in one's life. Life is to flow along naturally, people are drawn to you because they see you move effortlessly and want the same for themselves.

So awareness, taking action if needed to better a situation by being mindful as well as the reaction or non-reaction to things all play a part in emotions motion.

Power Of Thought

Thought is powerful

words cannot be seen,

but visible in the

mind of imagination!

Thoughts– words are powerful! From the conception of thought this invisible energy does go somewhere. Whether one holds on to thought, themselves or it is shared, it is an invisible energy.

Something will be created in some form, some way.

Which it is why we should consider all thought. If it is of a 'positive nature' that would be a good thing, a beautiful thing!

If it is of a 'negative nature' one may want to consider strongly before releasing and sharing it because it may have consequences to some degree by its expression.
Every spoken word does have a consequence
with its expression!

continued

How we refer to things-people-deeds and so on make a big difference, the choice is all our own!
This is why . . .

Thought is powerful

words cannot be seen,

but visible in the

mind of imagination!

Empower

Look into your heart, inquire within
as to what you believe in.

Think, research, study, come to your conclusions.

Arrive to a place that you are certain about your beliefs.

You don't have to agree with everyone about everything!

Be your own thinker. Your heart is similar to your mind.

It will also tell you whether you are on track with your
thinking or not.

Think deeply about matters but live light hearted a life

allow others to believe as they may. Force nothing!

Be at Peace and wish the best to all . . . Empower others!

inspiration

Cocoon

Inside cocoon

        all is well

                outside is fine

      inside I thrive

all better seen

      by sight sound and smell

           clear vision clear image

     from inside this shell.

The Maze

Life is good in all phases

in all stages in all ways

as I make my way through

this maze nothing can stop

me because even blindfolded

I know I will eventually arrive

to my destination with no hesitation

I'll take the self challenge then manage

all turns through this maze of it all!

Being

If you are coming into your belief system or have been there for quite some time and are comfortable 'just as you are' being an effective, productive contributing member of society 'being' of the human being race . . . Congratulations! You're a winner in my book of 'God Loving Loved ones'!

You see, someone has to tell you because you deserve to hear it! You deserve to hear all the wonderful things anyone would like to hear just for being yourself, a loving person!

'So where's he going with all this stuff' . . . (you think to yourself)?

Well, I'll tell you! I find it just a bit strange when someone says to me "you're this or that" or whatever they 'want me to know' what conclusion as to whatever 'they feel– they think I am', you know the division thing that separates us– one from another . . . the 'them and us' thing! . . . it can creep into everything sooner or later.

To me 'fellow man' can at times seem more concerned about me and mine than himself and his own.

Now where was it I read "judge not least ye not be judged" . . . hum? I know it couldn't be in "How to Date for Dummies", I know it wasn't in "Mad Magazine"! . . . 'ahh yes' it was the Bible! Or the good book as they say.

Speaking of Books, 'why this is a good book' as well, wouldn't you say? I thought you would!

People read a lot of different good books but I at times find it strange when they forget some of the goodness, the good

continued

thoughts of not letting the differences or what they consider to be 'the differences of others' get in the way of a friendship– relationship by making statements and judgment calls is my thought for the moment. If I find myself in that position it's because someone has given me good cause– reason to think 'just where are they coming from'? It could be of the unfair treatment we sometimes are to deal with of others, talk. I know the least I judge, the more time I have to do what I actually need to get done and that's to be productive in some way!

It's interesting to see how just three of the very basic 'negative destructive things' man can resort to that interfere in relationships. One, pre-conceived notion or judgment of others who someone may be, or may not be. Two, useless negative 'gossip' about someone to others of what they perceive. Three, the unfortunate idea of spreading any one of these to perhaps even creating rumors of someone that land in the lap of the gossiping, judgmental ones, that just serves no one at all.

I see this type of negative destructive thing as to interfere and damage relationships all coming from an unsettled, un-centered spirit, not fully aware of itself or on the other hand not aware and maybe not caring of the consequences created. Creating discord, disharmony within parties which doesn't make the world go round any better!

If one finds themselves in this position (finding yourself recipient of this treatment) there's really only one positive solution . . . rise above it! If you truly know what you place in your heart, resort to that. Only you know who you are and what your well meant intentions are. I don't control anyone 'but I do guide myself as best I can to create a little thing I call peace which understanding follows.

Reason

There's a reason for living, you decide?

                A purpose for giving you will find.

This reason for living it's found everywhere.

                In hearts to hold, our love is to care!

Life's more than a dream with scenes yet untold,

                Keep searching, keep looking as you get old.

respect

Heart Mover

Earth mover earth shaker medicine man.

Skywalker heart mover move as slow as you can.

Dream catcher love maker love fellow man.

Give

It's

Not

What

You

Get

In life

...

it's

what

you

give!

Who?

Who are you . . . how are you?
There's value worth to give new birth to a new idea– new thought,
Something of sweet desire!
Create brightness to your days, come out of that ho-hum haze,
Start in small ways, guide your mind guide your heart!
Cast aside that someone owes you something, is to do for you, or is to provide for you.
All are on equal ground here in this life, each does for themselves.
Unrealistic expectations are just that . . . unrealistic!
God spirit and universe support and provide for me well!

Who are you . . . how are you?
For a moment place aside that you are to achieve.
We are made up of so much where's sky's the limit. We are provided for in so many ways but it won't be discovered until one broadens their horizons and that may mean switching tracks as well as stopping the train all together and enjoy the view, both the inner and outer of you.
Enjoying the view is 'key' to living well, staying in tune with nature . . . your nature!

continued

Who are you . . . how are you?

Doing is good– doing is fine, just being is a chance to see just how far you've

come and how you're moving along and where you are to go.

Tap into your heart, feel the beat of your heart pulse beat for a moment and be a part of everything as well as the nothingness that surrounds you.

That's also there where you'll find who you are!

Flow Free!

Never allow yourself to feel sorry for yourself! That might be viewed as being a victim of sorts, or self pity. Instead in that moment shift the focus on the ones less fortunate, the ones going through situations far more challenging than what you may be dealing with, cultivate compassion. Remember 'your health is your wealth'! So is every one else's health.

Take command of the moment at hand . . . Do! Do! Do! something instead which requires your attention far more greater than how you might see yourself in that moment, a victim. There are things to get done that require our attention.

We have a responsibility to ourselves, for ourselves but also to one another. A warrior goes into battle knowing he is to succeed as opposed to 'hoping he will succeed, and there's a big difference.

Looking at oneself as a 'victim of yourself' or because you think 'someone has made you so' has no value. Are you a victim or victorious? By being victorious I am referring to dealing with matters– situations from a higher light. Drawing from ones best thought 'higher thought', to see the circumstances that occur have a better outcome, all done with a certain grace.

Do that which helps you gather yourself together to weather whatever storm of emotion or circumstance that is in that moment.

Staying fixated on the situation at hand can only 'lock you– freeze you up', lingering there can further complicate this

continued

moment you may be struggling with. One loses a sense, a certain 'free-flow' of life. Life is about movement, feeling like one is moving forward, being in a moment one naturally flows forward. Victimization has no value.

Attention to even the smallest detail 'other-things, other-needs' that need to get met requires action, time is better spent there.

Eventually the dilemma of the moment will subside– pass along and three basic things occur. One, 'we don't waste time locked up– frozen in time with self pity. Two, 'Other things' that need to be attended to get met. Three, 'We train' ourselves to be better in the moments of our lives guiding ourselves along being effective in a day.

Self guidance through self initiative one experiences 'peace' self peace, which 'all good things' are born of, an understanding of things, how things are.

Self mastery looks and feels much better, 'and is' than wallowing in self pity– despair within self sorrow.

So allowing yourself to feel sorry for yourself, feeling less than good or well, simply has no place within any one.

grace

Birth Of Life

Mother of my birth

    what reason is this life worth?

        for it is not to view

            the suffering of others.

                the pain inflected

                    by some

upon others, no!

    but to delight in life

        all the while the birth of life and that,

            the birth of a child.

Seize Your Power

You have the power
and ability to recreate yourself.
This quality is within you
as a matter of fact
it is expected of you,
it's by divine design.

This energy is all within
waiting on your
direction to guide it.
There is a certain energy
awaiting your arrival

to guide it to your heart's desire.
No one can take this vision energy
from you but it can be stifled
by your non belief in your power,
capture and . . . Seize your power!

Love Joy

Talk to me

God spirit

of earth

sky high.

Speak to me

beyond the winds

of hearts

dancing free

that my mind's

eye might see

moving freely

with love joy

in their hearts!

Consider Stress

In the mid to late sixties, early seventies, stress was a very well mentioned topic. Self-help books spoke much about the concept of stress within many a book, it was a topic of that era. It's an issue that will always be at the forefront of minds of healers, as well as the medical profession and for good reason, it can affect the lives of individuals, families and society.

Stress can and will in fact play a part in the lives of anyone– everyone to some degree. I'm sure you might have some reading material that addresses this topic and might be aware of this yourself.

I can't let this important issue on stress go by without sharing my views on it with hope that it may reach even one person who could benefit from it.

I have been in the music profession for quite some time and this industry has its share to deal with like other professions do as well. Stress can be off-setting, unsettling, and at worst mentally crippling and it can even work its way into other areas that it may trigger further negative responses to further set one back.

All of the human body is connected to all of the human body!

I believe it's to our benefit to be reminded "refreshed mentally" to basic life effecting concepts that keep us moving forward or in the present moment. With this piece

continued

I'd like to share information and ideas as to why one may find themselves stagnant or spinning wheels and not feeling like life isn't moving along.

First of all 'positive energetic people attract– positive people'!

Factor in the aging process. As we age we tend to lose power, energy and possibly the desire to deal with certain re-occurring situations that do effect us directly in ways that we may find 'off– setting, un-settling, and perhaps mentally crippling'. Consider this fact when dealing with elder family members, friends and also in personal loving relationships, and in work.

This is an area where many of the "up and coming into their own" in the work force are aware of. Classes in Yoga and Meditation are now everywhere not only to promote good health but the benefit to de-stressing are directly addressed there as well.

I believe stress can manifest in two ways. From the inside of the body outward, as well as from outside inward.
What I'm referring to is consider this . . . Stress– tension from the outside inward, 'outside of yourself to now inside yourself' from an encounter with another, or some tragic event which may have happened.

Let's say some one engages you with a certain negativity it may be 'how they are' delivering a certain thought, opinion, or whatever and it doesn't sit well and you in turn aren't doing well for whatever reason you may have and

continued

over react or meet negativity with the same negative response as a defense.

The situation may get magnified, blown-out of proportion and now things seem to get worse and you are stressed, tense, off centered and just not feeling or doing well in that moment.

If you were relaxed, centered at peace it may not have triggered an over reaction from yourself 'which is key' in being effective in relating to that person or anyone else. Also remember things subtly develop over time when we don't attend to ourselves and understand the nature of this energy, the concept of stress.

I have a saying 'you don't have to go out and look for trouble at times, it will come and find you'!

Remember, we are really only responsible for 'ourselves' and not the other person; think this thought through!
My message is "it is in how we react", out of control or in control?

In my first book "Love Endlessly" I mention on many topics that affect us throwing oneself off balance. Stress can trigger hurt, anger, resentment, old unresolved issues that weren't dealt with in the past and could cause health issues that affect us and those around us.

We are responsible for our own. Like in the lyrics from a song which went– "God Bless the child that's got his own"– I'm referring to 'self under control', or 'is doing well'.

Now on the stress from the 'inside out', from 'inside one self to outward'. I am referring to physical tension or stress that one may carry and not even consider it as being a factor as to how you may be relating, communicating with others.

Now I'll use exercise– working out as an example- as much as I am big believer in exercise– weight training one may not consider 'the after effect' that may be or exists after a workout session when you don't stretch afterward.

Plain and simple it's tension, muscle tension, stress.

I use this as a good example because it can also effect the nerves and joints in the body, maybe create impinged nerve 'a crimping' of the nerves that effects blood flow. Stretching is very important after a weight training session or any given exercise.

Now you can see from these two examples the importance of attending to stress; it's affect is far reaching than one may imagine.

compassion

Windsong

Windsong speak to me

sing to me

sing me a story

sing me a song,

I'll let your breeze carry me

move me along

I have all day, marry me

let your melody sing to me . . . a sweet

Windsong!

God Spirit

Tested at almost every turn what lessons will I learn?

I yearn to learn from this heart of mine.

To succeed getting more done doing less I must

confess seems to be the way.

My actions I see must be arranged to fit

is what I find. A test at best is just a quiz.

What choice what way– how will I act, what will I say?

I know if I pass– if I go far there won't be any golden star

but to know I'm on track with nature, a loving force.

A test came my way I passed with flying colors . . .

God Spirit led the way!

No Thought

In the silence of my mind all is a peaceful calm.

No thought occupy's this quiet space only timeless time exist.

I am this space within as well as the space outside that surrounds me.

Slowly I am becoming aware of this space that surrounds me.

This is because of the white light that surrounds me with all I long to feel.

The peace and tranquility that I sense are the inner and outer worlds

that I am comfortable with because all is always well in my world.

Going to this space from time to time is natural and life giving– life understanding.

I am the peaceful calm that exist and share it with others.

Ego

I'd
rather
be
caught
driving
a
yugo
than
to
ever
be
seen
behind
the
wheel
of
an
Ego!

Visionary

A visionary is someone

with a good sense of balance of mind.

One who you might say has his finger on the pulse

of things well enough to have a sound opinion on things.

Someone who has contemplated the past, thoughts of the future but is here now!

It has been said that the mind will regulate itself with old useless information and allowing for new

important information to be stored– used in it's memory bank. As a musician we play in the

moment as well as project into the future. We look ahead or listen closely as to where

the song is going to add our part as we move forward. This to me is an important
thing to develop.

continued

Being in the moment

and consider projecting forward.

Artists are visionaries, seeing works of art into form-shape before completion. As humans we all have this ability naturally. I believe it's important to cultivate it and let this work for you, draw upon it as you need it and let it work for you.

selfless

Fearless Or Fear Based

In my first book *Love Endlessly– a book of insight to inspire*, I touched on understanding the body language, our own as well as in others. Knowing how to basically read it. I believe it's important to understand it at times in others because it's to be a benefit in relations– relationships. At times people can say what they wish to talk about, this or that and there might be something 'not fitting' which 'one may' want to consider. But there are many reasons I would like to share for a moment more on this.

Eye contact would be the first to understand, there's so much in basically connecting or not. Initial eye contact speaks at first. Personally I don't care to force anything, if someone doesn't care to connect that's fine, but if they do I will know it! A smile is soon to follow which says something, it could say 'hello from across the room' or just be neutral and not speak.

Arms can speak as well crossed arms could say 'stay away' or 'I'm angry or maybe– I'm judging you, your appearance, the way you may be dressed? The phrase 'with open arms' can say so much like welcome! Body posture could say 'standing slightly' twisted off to the side (torso) slightly at an angle at times one could maybe saying– 'I'm shy' or be saying 'I don't care to talk much'!

Note always the tone of voice, this can be a little tricky and may require a bit more in understanding. How someone refers to things, from what language– words being used, to what they may be affirming to.

continued

This to me is important in communication, being effective is important in our lives, being positive or negative.

So why am I going here? Well I like to share what has served me which I don't neglect. I have many friends from different ages to different backgrounds. Some younger and have simply have not come into an understanding of the consideration and importance of this basic information.

Some people may know this and just live hectic, busy lives and fall out of touch with these concepts and it could very well serve them at the time of need; the other thing is– I am a people person, I love people and through my books offer the best of thought.

Now on to the other most important information I wish to share which is all in the title 'Fearless or Fear Based'. First of all compassion is 'first-primary' when concluding someone you see may not want to make or care to make, or be able to make eye contact at first sight.

Compassion is born of grace, respect, being sensitive towards others. You don't know if that person has experienced a dramatic situation– event and just doesn't care to connect, they maybe more than shy which is to be respected. And or someone just may be naturally shy to begin with. There could be a number of reasons.
Or you could encounter someone like myself who is very direct. I believe to engage with someone for myself I look them directly in the eyes, yes, I do allow myself to wander a bit afterwards because I know my energy is at times

continued

strong and might be overwhelming so I read myself and look around but return back to focus on the person I am engaged with, my friends know my vibe. But if I have to make an important point 'I stay fixed'!

The 'other side of the coin', as they say, is you may encounter someone eager instantly or naturally wanting eye contact and from there things proceed naturally comfortable for both.

Want to know more about body language simply study the actions of others anywhere, cafes or just anywhere in public and access it for yourself . . . sky's the limit! Study your own body language as well.

What energy do you have, what do you carry? Consider two important things, 'Fearless or Fear Based' energy? This can vary depending all in a day. Depending on your involvements for the moment, how your day may be going.

I'd like to think I carry and do my best to keep a balanced energy. Not fearful but I more work at being considerate towards others. Being sensitive toward others as well as myself. On fearlessness I go into situations with 'open eyes', an open mind as much as possible.

If I think someone is in a place of what I expressed earlier I handle things as best I can not to make anyone uncomfortable with me and the reason is I know I can be very direct which I know can be 'off setting' for some people.

continued

Make no mistake I don't consider myself grander stronger or any different than anyone else, but I do work at understanding myself as best I can to simply be an effective person 'contributing to life in my own way'.

We all go into situations wanting to connect with others, you could say, to win one another over. Things are much better when we connect naturally free flowing.

To have a basic knowledge of basic concepts does have it's advantages.

And really in the end relationships are also an opportunity to learn about ourselves. How are we acting or reacting in situations.

Grateful

I'm

    fortunate to be

        where I am in this season of my life

            I am grateful for all that has come my way.

I've

    always managed

        to overcome the challenges that have come my way.

        With good intention and effort things are

            getting done!

gratitude

Angel Eye

Have you ever kissed an Angel?
Have you ever held her so close felt
her warmth and thought time was standing still?

Have you gazed into the soul of her eyes
as you both lay side by side with pure love
running through your veins?

Have you ever wondered if she
knew or felt just how deeply you truly loved her,
and what she meant to you?

Have you ever had pleasant re-occurring dreams of her?
Dreams that were sensual to even highly intensely
loving sexual dreams of her that held you in a
moment not wanting to

awaken from dream state, slowly
moving through time in a vivid blissful
moment of 'this is really happening' and

I want her to feel what I'm feeling?
Have you ever blessed that angel time and time
again even after the fact she had
to leave and move along and go
away? . . . I have!

To My Lover

Love you can't
hide from me
I'll always find you.
Then let you go freely
because that's
how I found you.

My wishing well
is full of you.
I know where
you are.

You're in between
this world and another.
I know soon
I'll give more to you,
more of Love,
and to my Lover.

Golden

Getting older and feeling so much more bolder,
There's no stopping me now! I always knew life's colors would
change from blue to a bold golden gold as far back as I began to grow.
What's bold you ask? It's big-bright-brilliant-resilient, it's how you feel think inside.
An energy that just can't hide! It's okay to be-think-bold we were given this gift so long ago.
Some seem confused while others grow a bold-en golden bold!

The human spirit wants to like, wants to love naturally
also receive the same! This spirit wants to know it is operating from
A place of order born of Love! That it is appreciated simply for how it is, that it is!
It wants to give–seeks to live! It's on an endless quest to find-connect with God Spirit within
another's smiling face. To trace the 'beauty of life' and promote it rightly so.

continued

To lose a golden shine over time may be a sign,
looking outward and beyond not inside is where one really resides.
Keeping a balance, there's nothing selfish to look-go within, that's where life begins!

To care and guide ourselves along there's nothing wrong caring for the you that regenerates from a dim shade of gray to
a bold shade of gold. The stars shine bright, the sun is sun-yellow-gold, the moon if all a glow into the night . . .
as you are bright golden gold!

The Trap

The negative effects of substance abuse can be managed and over a period of time possibly be eliminated altogether! For some with a history of prolonged usage professional help may be the 'only way' to combat head on! Rebounding from substance abuse is just around the corner from a life thrown off its natural course "off track" due to usage.

With constant loving energy to guide it 'things will in fact change for the better'! When you think of it does in fact get down to a day to day focused energy to conquer substance abuse, it's affliction. Not until being honest with oneself and admit that one in fact does have a problem and takes action, nothing will change! Over time one may lose faith and belief in oneself, attitude demeanor and drive as well as energy diminishes. One may become less caring relations begin to struggle and more challenging perhaps even fail.

Anything that hinders- effect loving relationships deserves to be looked at closely! True change day to day even moment to moment does require a focused energy. Prescribed medication, drugs as well as alcohol all sooner or later effect in negative ways. I group alcohol in this because of its highly toxic effect but mostly because of its social accepted usage, it's accepted and therefore can easily turn into habit forming.

Simply put alcohol, drugs, substance abuse do take the shine off of person slowly over a period of time, it dulls a

continued

person's spirit, the sparkle in the eyes, but it can do so much more, damage to others around them. If you think you have a problem "now would be the time" to address, conquer and over come it!

Falling into the trap of substance abuse is at first subtle over time. Caring less and less can begin to take place. Hang-overs can over time turn in to hang-ups, problems relating with others. This can happen before one is aware or even realizes or for that matter could even imagine!

On the other hand when addressing the issue, a re-newness to one's life begins to form and things slowly fall into place. The human body will in fact heal itself but it first needs help to get it on track.

If you see yourself here within this writing know you are more powerful than you may believe or know! You have the power to first "set your mind" on that which you see as your aim and turn it all around. You hold the key to the door of your life. I wish you well!

balance

Love

Love is sacrificial, it is humbling

      It sacrifices hurt and anger,

            it is all giving all of the time!

Love is patience, it is nurturing.

      Being loving helps progressively

            to change the world for the better.

Aside from warming the heart noticeably

      love draws others to you.

            Love is caring, giving and forgiving

Love is the most

      powerful positive emotion

            we have to share!

Beauty Of You

May good fortune find you first!

May the eyes of another look upon you and see the beauty you possess!

May the days of your life welcome you warmly!

Traveler

In a way

it would be

sinful

To

turn

away

and

not

to

welcome

A

traveler

down

life's

road

in

search

of

himself!

Night Blue Yonder

Glued to the cell of the phone?
I thought the scent of my cologne
might keep you off the phone you know the electric bone.
But that might be a distraction from all the action
happening out there in cyberville.

After all how much information
can you get in a day? If you ask me there must be another
way to 'woo you',
the musk must make you think I have an ivory tusk?

Communication breakdown is the only thing I see here.
I just want you near, all this viewing back and forth on a
scroll is just getting
old and we're on a date. I can't wait till this night fades
away into the night blue yonder.

persistance

Just Live

If someone tells you this isn't a short life they simply aren't seeing the truth! This is a short life indeed! We witness the slow transformation of ourselves and others in time. The birthdays that come and go, the passing of family and friends making their transitions. The years and decades that seem to sweep by and we wonder 'wow' time is really moving on, and there's so much yet I want to do!

Time begins to close in. But we have been chosen to give-gracefully this day in all ways. As we age and come more into 'our own' we begin to understand things– everything much better. Things become more clearer. We understand ourselves and others better as well. There may be those that think it is a long life here instead maybe because they are bored. Maybe bored with themselves perhaps their work, their spouse any number of reasons, and have simply lost the excitement of living, the joy the fulfillment of it.

Or maybe some are simply unhappy and not content, and not making an effort to change as to help themselves along. To offer themselves renewed life by guiding the course life is on. There are any number of reasons one may think this is a long life. Perhaps it feels like life is possibly dragging along slowly and not doing anything about it, I can see this from their perspective.

continued

A pessimistic view on things on life itself could be possibly the reasons for this mindset. Perhaps there's a 'why bother' negative mindset in place holding one back.

But each day should be one of something to look forward to. Create something of excitement to look forward to. Writing does it for me. I enjoy receiving concepts– thoughts to think through and express whether it be with poetry, songs, or capture my thoughts. At times some of my best and easiest to express come to me just after I wake up from naps to wake up in the middle of the night or early morning and write. I touch on this in my first book *Love Endlessly, A Book of Insight to Inspire*. We create the life we desire. Our lives will take on the energy and form we give it, our energy level will be what we create it to be.

When we come into a clearer understanding as to who we are, what life is and our role in it everything comes better into play– view, a better understanding – truth! One is more content, fulfilled having made changes of some kind now and feeling well- better about themselves moving forward.

If you'll notice it's the ones that say at times 'I never want this to end', or 'if I only had just a little more time', those are the ones that see it as it is, time is short, life is short. All the more to live to the fullest 'Now' and truly not be concerned with how long it is to last. Just be centered content doing-living and giving.

This world is changing as designed in many ways. There

continued

are many coming into a better sense as to who they are and also how they are living their life. We are blessed to witness this in a collective way, therefore we create a better world for those that follow us as it is improved– we evolve. Reflect on the positive side of life and know the other exist but remain centered.

To sum this up. I believe that for myself it's found in self-improvement and being consistent with my spiritual practices, my spiritual work. And that includes being genuinely Loving, kind and respectful to all others. In being this way I give and therefore, I just live.

Out The Window

As we

  practice our

   spiritual

    practices-beliefs

     the door

      to understanding

      life, opens

       wider and

        wider, fears

       tend to

        go right

        out the

         Window!

Spirit

Well into my 'third act' now and in full
regalia and not concerned with curtain calls.
Truth is I'm naked as a jaybird and Love is the word- the message!
I've worked well keeping 'it all' together.

Weathered many a storm but not given more than others.
We all are given 'equally the same' here in the
game- the mix of life,
but never more than we can take.

The human spirit is so powerful than
some may know. It blooms moment to
moment as life goes ever more powerful. Faithful Loving
spirit destined to
move with more to give, graced in Love for all is meant to
be here.

Spirit

We'll rise up; third get now and in full
receive, and not concerned with unity...
Truth I... a mind to appreciate... reveals the words
moment.
(ye... take were...song it all together.

Words... Cannot... down but put... prominent than others.
We all are given enacks the same here in it.
in the Spirit of the...
but down upon truth we can take...

The final as spirit is renewed... than
some... secretly... it before... sentient to
modern as in... some a for more... were... Faithful, Loving
gifts doall gotten..
now with, and... What... faith Love, or all a modern is
be held.

flourish

Blade Of Grass

The wind

carries

my spirit

through the

blade of grass

to the seas.

I set

my sails

to be all I

long to be.

I see

far enough

to weather

any storm

ahead

eager to

share of my

Love.

Being Well

Be with those that life you up!
The ones that always tend to bring out the best in you as a person.
Be with the ones that you know you can rely on, not necessarily the ones that can
do things for you but the ones 'you know' that truly know and care for you.

They are the ones that look forward to seeing
you genuinely.
You can tell who they are because they tend to light up with a sincere kind,
loving love energy and make you feel welcomed always!

The cliche saying 'you can count your friends on one hand' holds truth!
At times some just seem disingenuous and may put up fronts that seem convenient
for the moment and you may not truly sense the true care and respect for you.

The fact is some tend to use others for their benefit- gain.
Trust your instincts, your intuition. When people are 'in tune' and your chemistry mesh well
things move along well and all seems right-fine-free-flowing.

Those that truly like and care for you always show and give you respect!
Remember we all are responsible for our well being, when things seem hopeless and perhaps
run its course it may be time for a change.
We are to provide for our own well being.

A Broken Heart

To thrive on in a world where heart break can over take one requires a consistent total loving energy, a focused love energy to see this through. The loss of loved ones usually triggers the onset of a broken heart, "a very real thing" many will tell you so! To preserve and 'keep on keeping on' requires work. Everything in life is earned!

Faith, prayer, belief, hope, effort, drive, determination, and a conquering spirit all must come into play! There are different losses in life, but the loss of loved ones tops the list! Our loved ones would want us to "thrive on word and live out a fulfilled life" because life supports life in all!

Besides the suggestions I mentioned, sound mental power (Peace), good nutrition, physical exercise, rest, seeking and being with good friends that are of a nurturing spirit, work, keeping active, contributing for the greater good of all play a part in letting time heal the heart! Stay strong in mind, with Peace in heart!

Forever

In my lucid mind I see you,

        pleasant warm is . . . your smile.

My arms stretched out for you

        eager to embrace you.

I sense your welcome.

        Together we will return to forever.

The Colonel

Gone is a friend whose memory
will live on in the hearts for many a musical day!

Blessed to have known you and your unique way to shower
many a friend,
always welcomed me in a wide-eyed-wacky way!

For you will be missed!!!

Rest in Peace Musical Warrior Co. Bruce Hampton

Dedicated to Atlanta Georgia's own Music Warrior!. . .
I imagine you, Ricky and Billy are going over the set list right
about now!
The stars are shining brighter now!

The Colonel

Colonel, a friend whose auctioneer
voice has meant to me many a musical day

I salute you and your unique never-changing
way of life
welcome the strawberry – blueberry fan

for you will be missed!!

Rest in Peace Marshal Warrior O. Boice Hamilton

Dollie did... Athletes Olympic Swimmer Woman.
I miss you. Bobcat Lilly gingerly over the spirits right
about now!
The stars are shining oh dear Lord...

positive

The Red Cloud

Looking

out beyond

an orange

red colored

cloud

where

grey

white

evening

sky

slowly closes in

I see

all

of

what

is

just

a

part

of

me.

In The World

Does someone see you

or does someone want to be seen by you?

Does someone like you

or does someone want you to like them?

Does someone need you

or does someone want you to need them?

Does someone own you

or does someone love you and want you free?

Does someone know you

or does someone want to know what it is you know?

Does someone want to be in your world

Or does someone want to just understand what it is to be in

the world?

Door To Your Heart

Let someone Love you but not let them steal your heart.

Let someone care for you, understand this is Love in its purest form.

Let someone give to you, giving is Love's sweet song a melody that lifts the heart.

Let someone help guide you to all the potential that you are.

For all of that which you are let Love open the door to your heart.

Mirror Facing Mirror

The imperfection of myself is just so perfect!

The imperfections of myself sparkles like a diamond!

The imperfections of others is like a mirror facing a mirror.

The imperfection of everything I see is so perfect.

Had I not discovered the imperfections of things, I would have little to work toward!

Mystical Sound

Sonic wonders
sonic sounds
from within,
your
vibration
makes me
grin from
inside out.
Mystical
musical
sounds
can turn
any upside
down frown
into something
more sheer
in delight
as tones
take flight
and catch
the wind,
something
that feels
good feels
Right!

pleasure

De la Terria

El Indio camina suave y despacio y able clarament.

The Indian walks softly and slowly and speaks clear minded.

Y ve lo que otros no ven esso lo que es importante . . . el Indio, the Indian.

El Indio es de la terria y vive despacio y save de suffrementios pero mas sabe como vivir.

The Indian is of the earth and lives slowly and knows of suffering but more knows how to live . . . el Indio, the Indian.

Camina suave y mida realidad de la terria . . . el Indio, the Indian.
Walk softly and see reality of the earth . . . el Indio, the Indian.

Golden Smile

Clear summer August evening,

    white tail hawk gliding by,

        sharing evening golden smile

            as smile meets sky.

"Toonces"

More than
just a few
ounces of kitty
Loving kitty joy
was Toonces playing
with a fur ball toy.

At nineteen
now moving on
to the 'great beyond'
to bounce and play
all the day
play on play on!

We will miss
you dear friend. . .
will you send
your Love
our way?

Dab a Grin

There's
    the power of love
        or the love of power.
            Which would you rather be?
Which would you rather dab
        on your head and rub that in
            that might make you grin?
Yes that's what I thought,
        you ought to keep that
            your focus on the most
power that does the most good
        and spread that
            for this world couldn't ever get enough!

A Kiss

If

I

could

Feng shui

my way

into your

heart

I know

we'd be

a neat

couple.

I mean

you seem

to be just

right for me!

I so much

want to

know you,

share the stars

in the skies

plant a kiss

on your cheek

as one shoots by!

Sacrifice

Consider doing whatever it takes within good reason to sacrifice something in some way to secure in getting-having-what you need for yourself. Bare in mind although people mean well and wish the best for you things won't change until one comes into the realization of knowing it will be by your 'well meant' efforts to create and direct what it is you need. Nothing should come at the expense of another, from using or taking advantage of anyone. God spirit and universe do not support that. We earn what it is we need. Your offerings will be noticed fully and will be cast in a 'proper light', your tree will 'bear fruit' by your attending to it. Proper seeds planted, along with the best fertilizer as well sufficient watering you can provide will make the difference. Interpret this as you will. Think how this thought might apply to yourself. We are given many days to develop and 'produce goodness the best' to even better as our contribution to life and mankind.

A basic law of nature is 'things become better and better over time'! So sacrifice may have to come into play when having to face and create a new direction knocking on the door. Giving up something could also mean making-

continued

creating a new space for something new to arrive and fit into one's life. We are living through a period in time where like in other times radical change has to take place. So change comes into play and sacrifice follows close behind to keep the flow-flowing-forward. Interpret this as you will. I could create and give many examples, scenarios as to what I'm sharing but just leave it there. So to finish up with this 'thought of sacrifice' for myself the fact remains it should be considered at times because when we do on the other hand 'we get' and have something to replace it with and life moves on. There will be 'a newness' a fresh new beginning. The idea is to be patient and stay positive with it all! Remember the universe balances itself out naturally perfectly.

energy

Heart

One heart one Love one mind.
  You Love because you love
    you give because you give
      you are because you are-
        Love made from Love,
          your Love is made from love.

            One heart one Love one mind.
          You care because you care
        you share because you share
      you are because you are-
     Love made from Love,
   your Love is made from Love.
One heart one love one mind.

Open Heart

When your

heart

is open

to giving

and

receiving

love

do

So!

The

idea of

not acting

on love

doesn't

always

seem

to come

around and

could be a missed

opportunity that you might not see soon.

With an open heart and open mind I choose the treasures to

give and take in time.

Respect

Respect is a powerful word yet it will make the biggest difference in one's life.

Self respect is respect for others. I wouldn't say I've lived a life so flawless with only ups and no downs, but I will say 'that which I've need to help me along has come to relatively well'.

And I am grateful for this!

I know besides a good faith effort I place in my work it's been because of being respectful toward others. I make it a point to show and give respect to others genuinely which I know makes the difference and opens the hearts of others.

I was taught to be respectful to my parents, family, elders, everyone and this filters into everyone and everything. I know it's a value that at times seems to have lost it's way.

This consideration comes right back to me by those that are of the same nature, the ones that show and give respect.

People want to be treated with respect they also want to give respect naturally, 'nature gives'! Man is basically good natured, giving is of a high order,

continued

it makes one feel good.

Nature provides everything, we are nature in human form. Life supports life! Respect is born of kindness, being kind- caring- loving- sharing- giving. Consider there are some that just don't ask for anything but need help or something, giving whatever in any way will make a difference, so if you don't have anything but your time. . . give that and watch what happens!

So "want kindness" show kindness, "want to be cared for and loved" give of all the same, "want respect"! Give respect and watch things just flow well in life.

Discover

Building on to this world-

this life is where I've arrived.

And to think so- discover

and know all was just under my

nose all the time.

Carrying less and less baggage

is one of the sweetest treats that

treats- me- greets- me

in the morning with that sweet silent sound of

pure nothingness.

If 'the best is yet to come' sure I'll take some . . . more!

'Victory'

I won't be life's victim!
I'll be someone who
will manage any challenge
that comes my way.

Victorious
yes I am!
I form my
plan at a
comfortable
pace then
execute
by means
to fulfill
my dreams!

There's
abundance
for
all
standing
tall.

You Deserve

Don't over think
it but do over dance
it and don't quit because
you deserve to move slide glide
into all that suits you well!

I mean I'm here to tell
you there's a world waiting
on your joy to come knocking so
start rockin and get your heart groove
on and make your mark and spread the love
and not leave a trail of tears but "of smiles" all the
while know you deserve the best!

Vessel

I am a vessel eager ready to share- care for the fallen ones.
The ones with hopefulness in their eyes.
They sit off to the side and watch others file in stand in line ready to order sit then dine.
You can tell they also just want to be a part of it all.
Why are they without?
It really doesn't matter now, but it doesn't change how they feel . . .
with out–left out. All they care for is to restore a feeling a
mode that seemed so long ago, one of simple nourishment, a feeling of being satisfied, content.
Sometimes my heart needs to break to remind me I am truly alive
as I thrive knowing others would like to be a part of everything- anything
even just to dine.
To feel like life isn't something passing them by.
They know every basic thing is for everyone.

continued

Some give up the hope and seem to just exist, you can see it in their eyes.
My targets are 'the chosen ones', the ones with the look of 'why even ask'?
They are the ones with hope fading fast, some never seem to ask, they are my chosen ones who light up with a sincere sense of gratitude,
I get an 'ahh' thank you and
God Bless you sir!
So blessed to be a vessel to know in time I can make some glow.
I can make some shine!
This world- this life is yours and mine.
If what goes around comes around
Let's create something Divine!

fearlessly

Moonbeam

I want to
be the moon
you beam upon
just before you fall
to sleep that leads
you to a
pleasant dream.

A note,
even a
heart
beat- melody
as it soothes
you to sleep.

The smile
upon your face
as you wake
back to reality
from dream.

I want to
be the icing
on your cake!

Golden Ones

A senior is a survivor!
An old warrior you might say, outwitting themselves and just that deserves respect!
At times outliving outlasting even the harsh ways of others.
Everything in life is earned and this they have learned time and time again!
They have crossed many a river and know the short cuts the best routes to take with the least amount of effort.

A senior can be a wealth of knowledge even speaking few words.
As one ages one tends to speak less think and listen and do more. So caution when around a senior for they 'hear' everything and take in what's important and just leave the rest for the chickens to feed on.

It would be foolish to underestimate a senior's demeanor.
A guide a teacher your best to confide in and they could just help you win!
Throughout my life seniors have been my best friends ever.
Their love patience and deep
Understanding of how things are have inspired me and guided me well.

continued

To my dear senior friends those that have moved on and those I'm blessed to share a moment in time with now . . ." this ones for you"! Because I know all too well that for you to arrive at the years you have had it's been well earned!

My love and respect to the 'Golden Ones'!

Affirmations

I cultivate the best of who I am and bring the same out in others!

I control my reactions to negative events- situations!

I am grateful for this wonderful life!

There's nothing I can't handle!

I have a conquering spirit!

Joy is something I create!

Dilemmas are short lived!

My Love last forever!

Peace is mine!

Heartfelt

When this life- my work has ended

I will have been at Peace with myself.

I understand man does suffer

but equally as important to me is of knowing we are

Blessed- gifted with this creation.

Endless opportunities have offered me many choices

to have lived a fulfilling life.

Through the imagination of my mind I give my heart to

those that suffer, but I only feel a part of their pain.

My prayer is, May they sense Peace and Love.

Smile

Little

sparrow

tweet me a song

tweet it so long

that I might fall

a sleep and dream

of the days

where time

was a

joy

filled

day

with

not

a care

a worry

with even

nothing

to say

but

Smile!

Responsibility

Being responsible means being accountable, being humble, respectful! It's understandable children can struggle in this area because they are still growing and learning. But at times adults . . . hum?

There will come a time it will be crucial in a person's life because it affects many areas in a person's life. I have a cross section of friends that I care for and at times I will place myself on the line to say what I think I need to share in this area to someone I care for whom I think may benefit from it and hope it is well taken, and I take responsibility for that!

Success comes to those that are responsible! Depending on what side of the coin of responsibility one is on, "things will happen for you, or to you"! Good opportunities await your being responsible! I have a saying which goes "take care of your business and your business will take care of you"!

There is a lot of truth in this saying. There will be times when returning phone calls in a timely fashion, correspondence. Even to showing up on time for work or a meeting or whatever the situation may be all require one to be responsible. Successful people always make themselves responsible and accountable to reap the benefits well earned!

Be Like Them

Often at times it seems like some

would like me to think like them,

see like them, be like them!

But some don't realize it's

way past 'too late'!

This horse already left

'the gate'

and now

making my way

around the track with

the score sheet tied to my back,

and almost at the finish line and ready

for a snack at the table in the stable!

Now rounding the final turn and in

typical 'slow-mo-slo-go'

form think I'll sprint this

one out and make

the score!

Rather

I

rather kiss

a stranger's dog

than to ever imagine

myself sitting on a log

with no friends!

I

rather sleep

in an old blue truck

than to even think

I was down on my

luck!

I

rather think

than drink my senses

away, that would be fine

that would be okay!

I

rather not

be in fashion than to

ever lose my compassion

for fellow man!

Warriors

Guardian- warrior always at the ready,
gatekeeper- peacemaker keeping all things steady!

A warrior is one who lays it on the line. A selfless one who clearly
sees his or her role- duty to serve country and nation. At times even to go
up and beyond the call of duty to secure turf and lives.

Most all nations have a front line of defense, a powerful one. And as we know there's
a side of man that will go to any measure to disrupt the peace and harmony of another's.
I am a peace Loving person but I am also a very practical man that knows this country should
be like many other countries, ready and able to defend itself in any moment,

No one really wants conflict, turmoil and definitely not war but we know man is created with
many sides of his being and at times chooses his ways of acting out. Let us remember an attack is

continued

quite different from a defense.

I am not confused in my beliefs but more practical in my thinking. So I say again . . .

Guardian- warrior always at the ready,

Gatekeeper- peacemaker keeping all things steady!

This is dedicated to the warrior spirit that fearlessly will place his or her life on the line to combat the sometimes evil, hustle way of man. Also dedicated to the families that know the loss of their presence.

Heart String

A selfless life that's where I'll go,
where what happens to my displeasure won't even get a yawn.
I'll look beyond and search for that which tunes me in and on, pulls heart strings has value
makes sense, has worth. To keep an eye out for the prize. . .
no it's not me it's in the sky!

Regret

I have always been someone cautious as to what I might say or how I may refer to things. For instance I don't use the word regret for certain reasons when talking with someone. I see this word as a ball and chain tied to around an ankle, it only can weigh one down even to the point of pointing the finger at one self of guilt of some kind.

Things in life at times are challenging than to further complicate and create guilts of some kind, I'm sure you might agree!

Besides 'I live in the now' not in the past gone by as much as I can which I couldn't change if I wanted to. If I make a mistake of some kind I do my best to learn from it, my part and not repeat it and just leave it there. I'm reminded of this word only if I hear it said or read it.

Regrets have no place in my mind, my thinking.

Develop Rituals

Focus on one thing at a time and do it.

Work at comfortable pace with a flowing energy.

Do it fully and completely, deliberately.

Do it with no distractions and no multitasking.

At times do less, don't overload your 'to do' list.

Place downtime in between things, reflect.

See progress!

Develop rituals, common set time to do certain things.

Serve others with gladness and not resentment.

Smile when you see good results from good efforts.

Smile for the sake of simply feeling good!

Keep an orderly space.

Clean and cook meditationally.

Think ahead, what is necessary to manage, deal with.

Live simply.

Of The Wind

Music

is the

sound

of the

wind

as it

whisk

through

the tree top

creating a sweet

whistling white noise.

Woodpecker tapping out notes,

a steady melodic rhythm melody.

All together nature plays its blend to mend.

Create Your Heaven

The saying is 'everyone wants to go to heaven but nobody wants to die'!
The 'great mystery' what happens after this life is what many including myself may wonder from time to time.
Life to me is so incredibly designed!
How things are, the knowingness of what's before our sight- our eyes to me is amazing!
Living a life in accordance with nature for me is the best way!
Understanding one's nature and the nature of things.
Witnessing
all the beauty life has to offer and knowing the reoccurring of it over and over speaks to me of how it doesn't end here. I understand that for those who can't handle or care to even think of the ending of this life may be a struggle to come to terms with. As I mentioned in my first book this is a mystery for me as well.
Again,
'I don't need to know everything' but I do need to be at peace with everything.
I need to flow with everything!
Rather than to be concerned with the fearful side of things, the fearful thought of passing on I say 'create your heaven' here and now! Being fearful about the unknown doesn't really have any place within anyone! Fear in a sense is born of not being fully in control of something, yourself, your thoughts. Guiding your thoughts in a positive light a

continued

positive way makes all the difference. Define your concept of heaven. Create your heaven here and now, share it with others and take a part of it when you pass and make the transition.

For life lives on!

Skyway

If I had a choice of taking the skyway or
the highway I'd take the skyway!
From high up out and beyond
I would see the back roads
and to just hear the toads!
At night I'd see the lights
of the village and small
towns, I would criss cross
the skies, man oh man
I would just fly!
I could see
the fireflies light
up the night all a
sparkling twinkling
glow to my eyes!

New Life

Death
you can't touch me,
you can't hurt me for you didn't create me!
Sorry to disappoint you but there won't be any pain when
you come knocking.

I'll just be rocking
in my easy chair staring
out to the heavens- my new home where I know

I won't be home
alone but with family and
old friends who will reflect on our visit here.

Wow!
Wasn't that a trip!
Most of it was cool and some of it was more
than I really cared for but I knew I'd survive just fine!

It's really nice
to see you all again, you sure have been missed!
I hope the others make it out alive without a scratch and no
one goes out kicking and screaming!

Death I know you're just a new life with a new face in
disguise!

Never Ending Dream

Some time we'll

meet again

in some form

or fashion,

some time we'll

meet my friend

life always

takes new action,

for me this dream

could never end

It's perfectly designed.

What's mine is yours

my friend,

what's yours

is mine.

Nubia

Nubia- Nubia you've gone through the fire, old self now

renewed.

New to touch the heavens with your light.

Now in a better place, great spirit smiles on you face.

Safe within this space.

Blessings unto you and your offspring,

may your children of three grow to sing

the phrases of being raised by none other than a good

mother!

Hamster Hop

Another wonderful power, packed day in this rat race that I'll turn into a one legged hamster hop from there I'll go into a crab crawl and finally work my way down to a snail slide that's where I'll slowly glide across the finish line and what a winner!

What an achiever with not even a master plan up my sleeve...
can you believe!

Keeping my focus eye on the prize I double reel myself in word as I at times let myself go outward into the mix of life! Yes this is all exciting conquering my desires, but looking for more has always been holding on the less and less of it all knowing I'll never fall.

They say 'life is what you make it', well if that's the key what I care to see is the sky, trees, hills, valleys and the sea. I want to see me kissing you, and you kissing me. I want to see you crying all over me as I lick every drop of joy hurt love laughter tears that move your being in love with life and me!

Marimba Medicine Man

A healer

    a tap dancing

        drumming marimba Medicine Man

            with healings of Love

    making his way through

the crowds.

For those in the know

    it would be hard for some

        just to let you go Dr. Bo

This is dedicated to my friend Dr. Bo Wagner, son, husband, father, brother, uncle, grandfather incredible musician, also co-founder of the popular Rock group Starbuck. Your spirit was always electric and full of fire. Now rest among the stars where you rightly belong and continue making the 'Moonlight Feel Right'. Rest in Peace dear friend!

Season

Friends this concludes the offering of this book. Just as life is an interesting beautiful experience there will always be challenges- dilemmas to overcome to work through and rise above. Problems will always exist in life. My thought message is you can go through life trading one condition for another that may have dilemmas slightly different than what we previously experienced but dilemmas just the same.

Man can go through life and think the 'grass is greener' on the other side or things are better over there but problems arise everywhere, this is the other side of the coin of living a fruitful life. We are also here to work through things, life. Everything is earned, our place-space here is earned and that goes along with everything. Relationships, jobs and so on.

My writings center on and reflect on the positive of mental mindset, being sound in thinking. Staying in touch- tune with positive thought. What this gets down to for me is 'much of it is about how it is we react to life's circumstances, situations events that occur.

I consider myself very fortunate and thankful to those that have enjoyed my two previous books (*Love Endlessly - A Book of Insight to Inspire*, 2014, and also *The Message*, 2016) which I have strived to share of my best higher thoughts. To offer a good food for thought. The kind

continued

sentiments expressed to me mean very much to know my thoughts and ideas can be moving to others and offer a sense of peace.

As I have said in the past 'I am in the best season of my life' now at this time with what I have learned about life and privileged to share with others.

When I reflect on the wonderful opportunities I have had, the blessings of family and friends that I care for I am truly grateful for this season. In reality it's not so much the opportunities, it's 'the blessing' of how I see what I have learned that's before my eyes.

To me life is so incredibly designed I can't help but reflect on it in positive ways!

I hope you the reader may take whatever good you can from it and it serve you well. And that all the seasons of your life be blessed!

In Peace with Blessings,
Luis Stefanell

www.ingramcontent.com/pod-product-compliance
Lightning Source LLC
Chambersburg PA
CBHW050642160426
43194CB00010B/1774